ICE AGE
COLLISION COURSE
Sticker
Scene Fun
AF251637
The Five Mile Press

A Colourful New World
Scrat's misadventures open up a wonderful new world of love and colour the Herd. Use the most amazing colours to finish the pictures below!
2

Let's Find the Love!
Sid has found his one true love! Help him through the maze to get to the lovely Brooke.
START
END
4

Sticker Puzzle

Use the stickers in this book to finish this puzzle.

Create a World
Imagine there is a wonderful, hidden magical world just waiting to be discovered! Draw what you think that world would look like in all its glory.

Make up
your own
fantastical
creatures!

Who is Who?
What a mix-up! Draw a line to match up each character to their correct name.
Manny
Scrat
Diego
Sid
Buck
A
B
C
D
E
8

Use these stickers for the activity on pages 12-13

Use these stickers to finish
the puzzle on page 5
Ice Age: Collision Course TM & © 2016 Twentieth Century Fox Film Corporation. All Rights Reserved.

Acorns Galore!

This is Scrat's dream come true! How many acorns can you count in the pile below?

I found
_____
acorns. YUM!

Floating in Space

Scrat has gone to great lengths to get his acorn.
Draw who else he might bump into in space next to him.

Odd One Out

Which picture of Diego is the odd one out?

Make a Scene!

Use the stickers in this book to make up your own
Ice Age scene with your favourite characters.

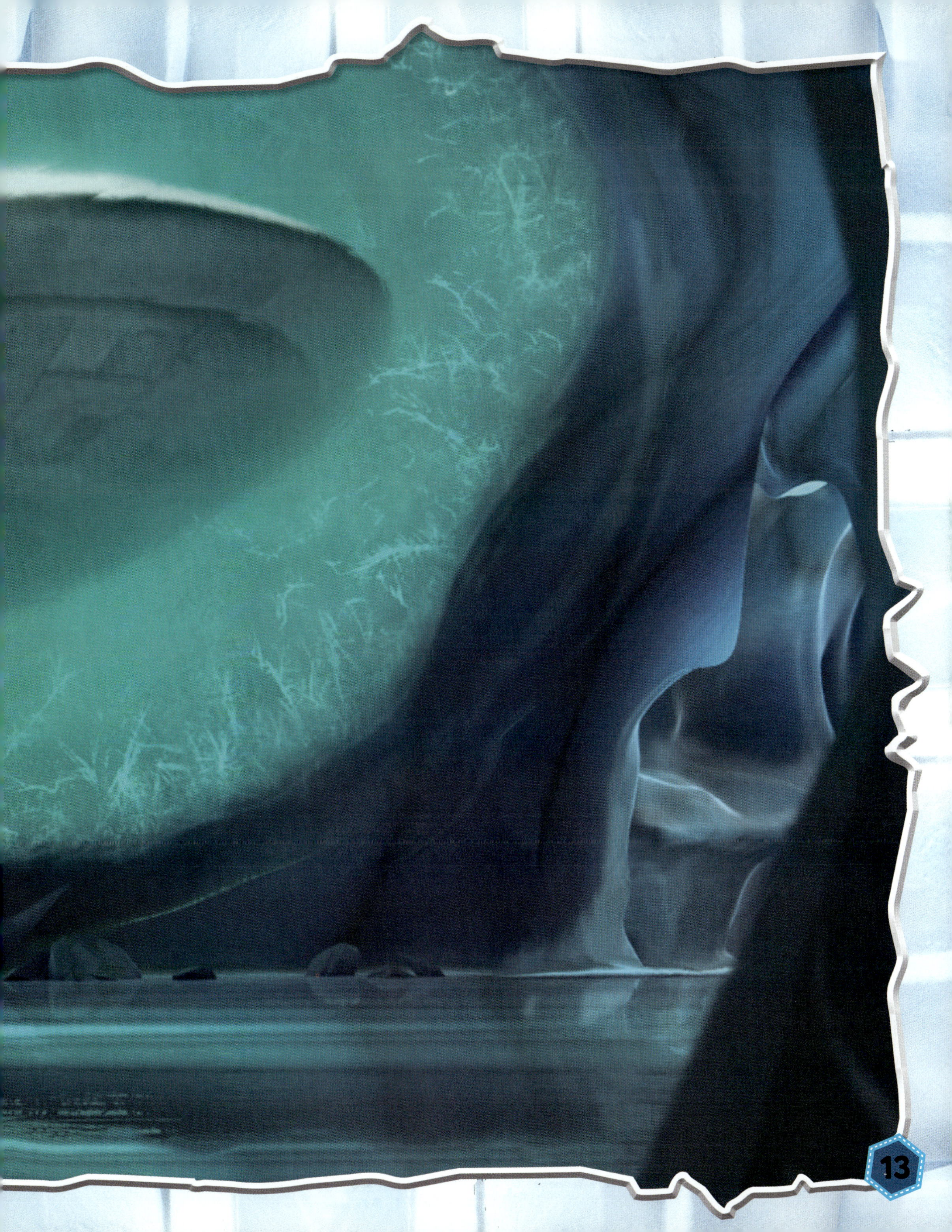

Cute and Dotty

Starting at number 1, join all the dots to finish this picture of an adorable little couple.

What is Different?

Look closely to find all six differences between these two pictures.

Answers

PAGE 4 – LET'S FIND THE LOVE!

PAGE 5 – STICKER PUZZLE

PAGE 8 – WHO IS WHO?

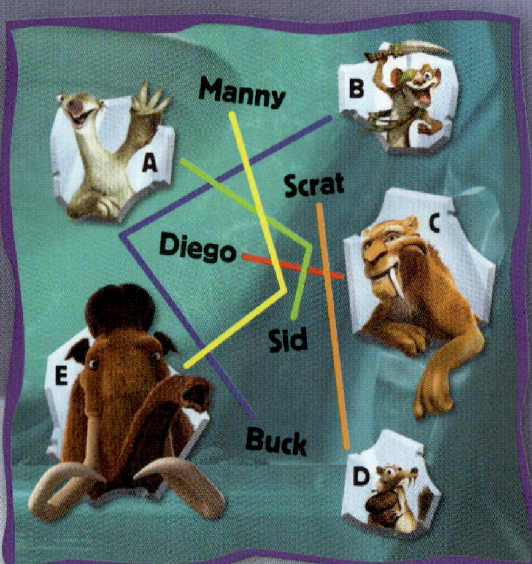

PAGE 9 – ACORNS GALORE!

There are 14 acorns.

PAGE 11 – ODD ONE OUT

C is the odd one out.

PAGE 14 – CUTE AND DOTTY

PAGE 15 – WHAT IS DIFFERENT?

1. Granny's walking stick is missing.
2. Shangri-Llama's jewel is now green.
3. Shangri-Llama's horns are now blue.
4. Brooke's fur is now pink.
5. Sid's tail is missing.
6. The flowers are missing.